The Heron Could Be Lost

poems by

Buff Whitman-Bradley

Finishing Line Press
Georgetown, Kentucky

The Heron
Could Be Lost

Copyright © 2022 by Buff Whitman-Bradley
ISBN 978-1-64662-858-2 First Edition
All rights reserved under International and Pan-American Copyright Conventions. No part of this book may be reproduced in any manner whatsoever without written permission from the publisher, except in the case of brief quotations embodied in critical articles and reviews.

ACKNOWLEDGMENTS

With thanks to the following publications in which the poems noted first appeared:

Bryant Literary Review—"If the stars had voices"
Buddhist Poetry Review—"Yellow mushroom"
Circle Show—"Lakeside Afternoon"
Coneflower Café—"A murmuration, December 2020," "Unglued," "The wild beauty within"
Evening Street Review—"Forest picnic," "Solo"
Fleas on the Dog—"Frog music"
NatureWriting—"December 24, Lake Lagunitas," "Friendly porch lights," "Special delivery"
New Verse News—"Another New Year's Eve," "Fat black bees," "New Year's owls"
Pinyon Poetry—"Inspiration"
Sheila-Na-Gig—"The heron could be lost"
Speckled Trout Review—"Birds of low repute"
Third Act Project—"December 26, 2020"
Walloon Writers Review—"The melodious silence of woods"

Publisher: Leah Huete de Maines
Editor: Christen Kincaid
Cover Art: Buff Whitman-Bradley
Author Photo: Cynthia Whitman-Bradley
Cover Design: Elizabeth Maines McCleavy

Order online: www.finishinglinepress.com
also available on amazon.com

Author inquiries and mail orders:
Finishing Line Press
PO Box 1626
Georgetown, Kentucky 40324
USA

Table of Contents

Special delivery 1
New Year's owls 2
Heron and turtle 3
Fat black bees 4
A murmuration, December 2020 6
Inspiration 7
Lakeside afternoon 8
December 24, Lake Lagunitas 9
Birds of low repute 11
Friendly porch lights 13
Looking for Chekhov 14
Pause 16
If the stars had voices 18
Forest picnic 19
The melodious silence of woods 20
All Hallows' Eve 21
December 26, 2020 22
Solo 23
Unglued 24
Another New Year's Eve 26
Yup, it's spring 27
How lovely we are in the woods 28
Frog music 29
Watching a ladybug crossing the fire road 30
Birthday poem 31
The heron could be lost 32
Yellow mushroom 34
The wild beauty within 35
Thank You 36

Special delivery

Spring has come to town
In its glittering blue delivery van
Stopping at each house
Up and down the street
To drop off packages
Of warmth and bright sunshine
And like children at their own birthday parties
Impatient to get at what's inside
We rip off the wrapping
Fling aside the lids
And when we lift our presents
Out of their boxes
They rise like kites and helium balloons
To fill the morning
While we gaze upwards
With pure delight
Giddily grateful
For these wondrous gifts
With no strings attached.

New Year's owls

In the first hours of the new year
After the midnight explosions have ceased
And no more revelers
In clutches of three and four
Go stumbling by the house
Happily jabbering away
I lie in bed with the window open
To the freezing night air
Listening to two owls
Speaking to each other
From nearby treetops.
Hu-hoo, hu-hoo says one
In a deep and quiet voice
Hoo-hu-hoo, hoo-hu-hoo
Responds the other
In a higher pitch.
I picture the baritone as an elder
Complimenting the young alto
On not panicking
During the booms and bangs and kapows
They had just endured,
On staying put in its tree
Until the onslaught of flash and bam had subsided.
It's safe to go out now
The old one says
But be mindful of the humans,
They are loud and messy
And really have no idea
What they are doing.
And of course the old hoot is right.
We are a cacophonous, lurching,
Bumbling, bungling bunch
Making a fine shambles of things
And we'd be a whole lot better off
If we resolved in the coming year
To cultivate a little quiescence
And pay closer attention to owls.

Heron and turtle

The heron walks ever so daintily
Along the half-submerged fallen tree
Being careful not to intrude
Upon the several turtles
Sunning themselves thereon.
But perhaps from being overly cautious
The bird makes a misstep
And bumps one of the lazing amphibians
Off the waterlogged trunk
And into the drink.
Realizing at once the consequence
Of its errant footfall
The heron launches itself up and away
Into the azure afternoon
Far from the opprobrium
Of the dislodged snapper,
While the turtle so rudely evicted
Hauls itself up out of the cold pond
Back to its spot in the sunlight
Sighing and muttering about the travails
A turtle's life entails
But so very happy to be warm again.

Fat black bees

A May morning
More like January.
I sit on the bench in front of the house
Brooding about the unseasonable weather
And looming climate catastrophe,
Wondering what it will mean
For our children and grandchildren,
For the children and grandchildren
Of all humanity.
Wondering if we will be able
To overcome the depredations
Of the mad, greedy bastards
Pumping ppms into the atmosphere
Day and night without pause,
With lethal, sociopathic glee,
Setting loose the wild dogs
Of hurricane and tornado, flood and fire
In order to stuff their greasy pockets
With mere money,
Not much good when everyone's gone.
Too late is almost here.
Will we beat the carbon clock
Or will we all be Ishis,
The last of our tribes?
And what about these fat black bees
I'm watching right now as they traffic
In the rosemary and jasmine
By the front porch steps?
Will they be able to adapt
To some fierce, inhospitable new normal?
Or will they follow countless other species
Out the door?
I dream of a fine May morning
A hundred or a thousand years from now
When our descendants
Will be lazing
In hammocks and lawn chairs
Appreciating the thrum and buzz
Of apian activity
As the heirs of these earnest little toilers

Arrive at the job site—
Blossoming rosemary bushes and jasmine vines—
Wide awake, scrubbed and shiny,
Ready for work.

A murmuration, December 2020

We stand, of all places,
In the parking lot of a CVS pharmacy
Just off the freeway
With hundreds of others
Gazing upwards at a spectacle
Of winter starlings by the thousands
Performing exquisitely fluid aerial calligraphy
In perfect unison
In December's pale evening sky,
Great liquid shapes
Constantly swooping and soaring
Wheeling and flowing and shifting
Coalescing, separating, merging anew
As some ancient
Air traffic controller
Guides their precision movements
From deep within their DNA.
We watch, struck nearly dumb
By the primordial pageant,
Able to utter only inarticulate exclamations—
Wow! Awesome! Unbelievable!—
And aim our phone cameras
At the firmament
To record this drama
Of the world creating itself
All over again.

Inspiration

Typically the ideas arrive unannounced
Often stumbling down the hallway
In the half light of dawn
Scratching their heads
Rubbing their eyes
Yawning and stretching and mumbling
Asking what time it is
And what's for breakfast.
I'll fry them some eggs
Or stir up a bowl of oatmeal
And after they eat I will offer them
The use of the shower
And whatever they want from my closet
Hoping that when
They are fed and scrubbed
Combed and clad
They will at least be presentable
In public
And might actually be someone
I'd be proud to introduce
To a reader who happens across them
While flipping through a small journal
Or clicking a link online.
But as helpful and supportive
As I try to be
They are often irascible and uncooperative
And turn out as rumpled and unkempt
And cranky
As when they first showed up.
And when that happens
Like a weary and long-suffering parent
Who's had it up to here
I breathe a deep sigh of disappointment
As I open the front door
And send them out
Into the difficult world
To fend for themselves.

Lakeside afternoon

Standing near the tip of the branch
Extending several feet out from its nest
In the dead treetop
The juvenile osprey is in a panic
Crying out urgently and ceaselessly
From its uncertain perch
High above the lake,
Will somebody please do something!

But no parent osprey appears
To offer direction or advice
Or even an encouraging word or two
About this monumental
And transformative moment
When a young bird will step off
Into thin air
For the first time
And must master aerodynamics
In a matter of only a few seconds
Before it plunges head first
Into the dark green waters below.

The frantic young osprey does not realize
That this absence of a backup crew
Is the ancient wild's way of saying
*You can do this on your own now, little sister,
No need for further assistance.*
But after more long minutes of plaintive pleading
An instant arrives
As it does in all our lives
When there is nothing else to do
But to obey the primeval instructions encoded within
To lift lightly off the spindly branch
Embrace the sudden plunge
Then blossom into flight.

December 24, Lake Lagunitas

Hiking the woods
In a good downpour
On the day of the eve of St. Newt,
Our slickers slick and shiny,
Our waterproof boots and socks
Soaked all the way through
To Mongolia.
Great puddles on the trail
Daring us to cross,
Jagged half-buried rocks warning us
Watch your step old-timers
You're just one slip away
From eternity.

Tonight is the night
Of the arrival of St. Newt.
Mushrooms jumpy with excitement
Pop up everywhere in the duff,
Downed trees and rotting logs
Are dressed to the stylish nines
In this season's mosses and lichens,
Creeks and rivulets and waterfalls
Are clearing their throats
As they prepare
To perform their hymns of welcome.
Out on the lake
Coots in small flotillas
Sail in and out of the reeds
Squawking without pause
Unable to contain their wild enthusiasm,
And a ceremonial merganser
Patrols a narrow inlet
With impeccable posture
And great dignity
As befits the arrival of the holy.

And the moment when the Anticipated One
Emerges at last from its sublime creche
Of decay and rebirth
The forest, the lake,

All vegetable and animal creatures,
Erupt in jubilant alleluias
In praise of St. Newt
And the angels of the rain.

Birds of low repute

On the sidewalk
Outside the café
There is a large metal bowl
Filled with water,
Placed there for the dogs
Accompanying their human friends
On a mission to secure
A hearty cup of java
In order to improve the day.
But alas just now
For the canine companions,
They find the bowl
Wholly and utterly occupied
By a bathing pigeon
Exuberantly splashing away
In the doggy water
And showing no signs
Of intending to depart
Any time soon.
What admirable critters they are,
These birds of low repute,
These avian scavengers
That clean up after us
And assemble in beautiful battalions
On the telephone wires and power lines
Of late afternoon.
They have learned to make the best
Of making do,
Finding sustenance where it is dropped
Or discarded
In gutters and alleys,
Vacant lots and busy streets,
Nimbly evading oncoming autos
That seem intent upon running them down,
Surviving municipal campaigns
To eliminate them entirely
From the civic scene.
Despite the meager esteem
And often downright contempt
With which they are regarded.

They carry on unruffled,
Showing up faithfully to work every day
In the refuse industry
And on occasion
Taking a few moments of well-deserved time off
For a scrub and a soak.

Friendly porch lights

Returning home
After an evening out
We pause on our way
Up the front steps
To cast a nervous glance upward
At the thick smoke
That has choked us
And the atmosphere above us
For days and days
And there we see
A few raggedy holes
Torn into the putrid miasma
Through each of which
A star or two dimly shine
As if signaling to us
From thousands of years distant
That there is always reason
To hope.
The omnivorous flames
Of an apocalyptic inferno
Rampaging two hundred miles from here
That for ten days now
Have been devouring
Forests and homes and lives
Continue to run amok in the countryside
Spreading oceans of hazard
Over thousands of square miles
As thousands of fire fighters struggle
To control the burning beast.
So we welcome this brief glimpse
Of friendly porch lights from far away
While we stand here
On Earth's great wide front stoop
Hoping for a few whiffs
Of smokeless air
As we shoot the breeze
About the neighborhood stars

Looking for Chekhov
     (inspired by the title of Joanne Townsend's poem "Somewhere near Odessa, 1900")

Somewhere near Odessa
In 1900, I think it was,
But possibly not,
You know how
In memory's paper bag
Everything gets jumbled together
And when you smack it with a stick
It all comes spilling out
Willy-nilly and higgledy-piggledy.

Anyhow, somewhere near Odessa
In perhaps 1900 or thereabouts
I boarded a midnight train
My portmanteau stuffed
With collarless shirts
And shirtless collars
One silk neck scarf
And my fine wool suit.
I was hoping, as you might not
Be surprised to learn,
To run into dear old Anton Chekhov
Who, it was rumored,
Frequently frequented
The midnight train running every other day
Between somewhere near Odessa
And somewhere near Moscow
In the neighborhood of 1900-ish.

You see, I wanted to tell Antosha
(If I might be so bold)
How very much I admired
All of his writings
And in particular how the shocking moment
In his story "In the Ravine,"
Soon to be published
(If it was indeed 1900)
When Aksinya pours a bucket of boiling water
Over the infant Nikifor,

About how that soul-shattering moment
Exploded and expanded in my head
Like a hydrogen bomb and its mushroom cloud
Until it became the size
Of all space and time
And how it remains thus within me still.

With no sign of Anton Pavlovich anywhere
I did some asking around and learned
That 1: He spent very little time in Odessa
And 2: He never once traveled on the Gorky Express
Between somewhere near Odessa
And somewhere near Moscow.
Deeply disappointed
I sagged into my first-class berth
With a snifter of brandy
And watched forlornly out the window
As occasional lights in the vast countryside flashed by
And snow began to fall all over Russia.
Somewhere in Moscow
The carriage driver Iona Potapov
Was telling his passenger
About the death of his son
As snow flakes settled into his beard
And tears froze on his cheeks
While the passenger remained oblivious.
Somewhere in Moscow
The exhausted servant girl Varka
Was trying to calm a colicky baby
When finally, desperate for her own sleep
She strangled the infant
Then sank deep into slumber
On a dreamless Russian winter night.

Pause

While the little girls
Play in the bedroom with grandma
I take the last batch
Of oatmeal cookies
Out of the oven
Then tread ever so softly,
So as not to be heard,
To the big yellow chair
By the big front window
And sit quietly
Watching the day
Make arrangements
For tonight's predicted rain,
Maneuvering vast gray clouds
Into place
And fitting them together so expertly
That not even a tiny sliver of blue sky
Is visible.
This is a sweet moment of pause
Which is unlikely to last
More than a few minutes
Until an eruption
Of 5- and 3-year-old virtuosity
Rattles the windows
And shatters the calm
To begin the next movement
Of a symphony of chaos
Requiring my participation
As jack-of-all-instruments
From xylophone to harmonica
To kazoo.
And although I am delighted
To make a guest appearance
With the rollicking girls' ensemble
I would not mind
Tacking on a bit more time
For this intermission
When, alone in the lobby,
I would be free to enjoy
My mental meanderings

As I contemplate the passage of time,
The meaning of life,
And the beauty of oatmeal cookies
Cooling in the kitchen.

If the stars had voices

If the stars had voices
They would surely sound
Like cricket song
Throbbing with passion and yearning
And tinged with melancholy
As summer's blue canoe
Drifts toward autumn.

If the stars had voices
We would sit every evening
Out on the front porch
To hear their fervent, achy airs
Just as we do now
In these tail-end days of August
Talking quietly about today's heat
And tomorrow's
And enjoying the hubbub and spectacle
Of whole galaxies of crickets
Twinkling in the grasses.

Forest picnic

Lunch on a log
Beside a tiny stream
In the midst of a forest
Of lean young redwoods
The water splashed and dappled
With whatever sunlight
Manages to make its way
Down through the canopy
The water tumbling over rocks
And through tangles of fallen branches
Singing to itself
Like a small child left on her own
To play in the back yard
And we the fortunate eavesdroppers
With the good fortune to overhear
The little one's shapeless, meandering tunes
Lucky to listen
To the lilt and murmur
Of free flowing water
That we will carry within us
To refresh us in thirsty times,
To lighten our spirits
With the memory of its song

The melodious silence of woods

In the melodious silence of woods
We listen for nothing at all
For the absence of snarling machinery
And the siren's strident call

For the sacred space where telephones
Are sweetly completely away
Where audio-video chatter
Does not invade the day

Where sylvan communal unquiet
Replaces the headlong rush
Where the calls of sparrows and scrub jays
Amplify the hush

Where a kingfisher's vivid screech
And the *crack!* of an oak's old bone
Welcome us to the hubbub
Of the silence that is our home

All Hallows' Eve

On Halloween night
As hordes of costumes
And their people
Prowl the streets
For sweets
A slender slice
Of moon
Floats
In the western sky
While nearby
Its celebrity sibling
Planet Venus
Is leading the way
Down the far side
Of today,
A jeweled cog
In the infinite machinery
That keeps the universe
On the move,
The granddaddy
Of all clocks
Ticking its tocks
Through the eons.
And those of us
With the good fortune
To have looked up
Just now
And caught sight
Of the two glittering sisters
Descending side by side
In the All Hallows' blackness
Are reminded once again
That there are more things
Horatio
Than bumps in the night
And the whoop-dee-doo flash-and-dazzle flights
Of migrating meteors
That can give us the shivers
And knock off our socks.

December 26, 2020
for Martha Noble and Lisel Blash

Well, it was a just a ghost
Of Christmases past
Families keeping their distance
Friends raising a glass
To all those
Temporarily or forever absent
Uncertainty and anxiety
Permeating the frigid air
Of the silent night, the holy night.
But more colored lights
Than ever before
Festooning trees and fences
Windows and eaves
Up and down the street
As if to say
Pause, look, listen
There are bright, luminous souls
Alive inside this house
There is music in these rooms
There is possibility
There is hope
Children are still being born
Jupiter and Saturn still repeating
Their immemorial conjunction
In the southwestern sky
Ruby-crowned kinglets and cedar waxwings
Still seeking bits of sustenance
In bare winter trees.

Solo

Eager for a solo career
The marshland frog quits
The winter glee club
And strikes out on its own
Across acres of muck and mire
And moldering vegetation
Until it arrives at the broad lawn
Outside the community center
Where it is busking now
In the vivid green grasses
Hoping to attract the attention
Of a passing Broadway producer,
A TV talent scout,
An operatic impresario.
But alas,
It is a thoroughly rainy day
And no pedestrians walk by,
There are only Grandma and Grandpa
Sitting in the building's roofed entryway
Waiting for the toddler in the stroller
To wake up from her nap,
And although they are great fans
Of frog music
Enjoying this performance tremendously,
And would be happy to help the talented tenor
If they could,
They are just ordinary folks
With no friends in high places,
No relative who knows someone who knows someone
Who knows someone,
No Hollywood princess to give him a kiss
And make him a star

Unglued

When insomnia
Drags me out of bed
After midnight
I sit in the darkened house
And listen to the papery rustlings
And whispers
Of the pages of books
Separating themselves
From their hard covers and bindings
And fluttering in ones and twos
Out the open window above the bookcase
Into the starlit night.
They will pass the hours until dawn
Wafting where breezes carry them
And exulting in the free-and-easy rambling life
Without any responsibility
For explicating the roots
Of a character's fatal flaw
Or revealing a terrible secret
Buried in augurs and inklings
In early chapters,
Of serving as an interlude of comic relief
Or as a particularly agile transition in tone
From the meditatively philosophical
To the stridently incoherent,
Or performing the thousand other tasks
They are called upon to execute flawlessly
Beneath a careful reader's gimlet gaze.
What a relief, then, to get away from it all,
Not to talk shop
With all the other pages,
To escape the fetters
Of context and story arc,
To stand on their own,
Be who they want to be,
Mean what they want to mean,
Until the first light of dawn
When they will return through that still open window
To reassemble themselves
And become bookish once more

Primly waiting in their assigned order
While they dream in secret
Of another fragrantly perfect night
To come unglued.

Another New Year's Eve

On a chilly December afternoon
A paper-white gibbous moon
Hauls itself over the eastern hills
Up through the seasonal haze
Into a sky crowded with pale, nondescript clouds
Shuffling between horizons.
A single winter sparrow pecks for seeds
On the ground beneath the grape arbor.
We open the doors and windows
To the cold air
And not without trepidation
Face those far hills
Where the new year will first reveal itself.
The future has twisted out of our grasp
And belongs now
To our children and grandchildren
To whom we must apologize
For leaving them to struggle
Against the tempests we might have prevented
But did not.
We cannot know if they will succeed or fail,
Cannot know if migrating geese and cranes and swans
Will someday not return
To the ponds and marshes
Where they have wintered for ten thousand thousand years,
Cannot know if the Great Mother
Will finally disown, disinherit and evict all her offspring,
The righteous and the not,
While this infinitesimal blue bubble once called Home
Just goes on wobbling and spinning
Through the oceanic darkness
Of the undivided now.

Yup, it's spring

Yup, it's spring.
Flowering in roadside ditches
Masses of mustard and wild radish,
Along with unruly crowds
Of wild oat and plantain
And other ornery grasses
That couldn't care less
What you think of them,
While in nearby fallow fields,
And vineyards still in repose,
Great yellow swaths of oxalis
Sway in unison
In the stiff breeze
Like diehard fans
At the Equinox Bowl
Cheering on the home team.
Acacias everywhere are going a little wacko,
Bursting suddenly and heedlessly into bloom
Without consideration
For all those sensitive souls
That their pollen will be tormenting
For the next several weeks.
And above it all
In the whiz-bang blue
Hawks in the throes of longing,
Poor dears,
Soar and gyre and ceaselessly cry
For someone to give them some love.

How lovely we are in the woods

How lovely we are in the woods
How nakedly glowingly green
How dappled we are with shadow and gold
How bluejay'd and rattler'd and bee'd

How liquid we are in the woods
How flowy and purly and clear
Like the creek that recites its watery odes
For no one at all to hear

How quiet we grow in the woods
How silent and deeply at ease
Receiving with bodily gratitude
The breathful blessings of trees

Frog music

Despite their natural exuberance
And their unmatched vocal virtuosity
In performing the masterworks
Of the great Jurassic composers
The busking frogs in the inundated bog
Cease their performance
As I approach,
A thousand voices braking simultaneously
On the same dime,
Reminding me
That there is an immemorial music
Humming and thrumming
Through the biome
And audible to us as the calls of birds
The howls of wolves
The electric whine of cicadas
The countertenor descants
Of the frogs eyeing me now from the mud
And refusing to resume their oratorio
Until they are good and ready,
For they sing only to praise the life within them,
They do not sing for me.

Watching a ladybug crossing the fire road

Ladybug, ladybug
Taking a stroll
Not in a hurry
Nowhere to go

Ladybug, ladybug
Ambling along
Basking in leisure
Humming a song

The kids are in college
She's needed no more
Why not take it easy
Go out and explore?

The house is rebuilt
The mortgage is paid—
Rent the place out
See the world, get away

But not via air
She's had quite her fill
Of flitting about
From river to hill

With six sturdy legs
And a bold heart untamed
She'll ramble and bushwhack
Low to the land

She'll have a great view
Down there in the dirt
Watch pill bugs skedaddle
And lizards cavort

Hike where she wants
From forest to sea
A vagabond ladybug
Footloose and free

Birthday poem

This morning I took my coffee
Out to the bench in front of our house
And sat chatting with my wife and the neighbors.
Many strollers passed by
And having turned 78 today
I was feeling magnanimous and a bit papal
So I blessed each one of them
Although not out loud.
This is the oldest I have ever been
And I am pondering
The contours of my new age
Trying to make some sense
Of what it all means.
It is early yet so I have come
To no definite conclusions
But I am getting an inkling
That I have at last
Achieved a certain gravitas
And will shortly feel free
To dispense advice willy nilly
Whether anyone asks for it
Or not.
Listen more, speak less
I will tell people I pass on the street
Or sit next to on the bus
Be patient, especially with children.
Practice large generosity.
Stay in the bike lane and
Walk your dog at least twice a day.
Think much, believe little.
Forgive.
Of course everyone already knows
All of this
But how affirming it will be
How reassuring
To hear these truths pronounced
By this kindly old gentleman
Who is so willing to share his wisdom
And who does not at all, by the way,
Look his age.

The heron could be lost

The heron could be lost.
It has flown slowly back and forth
Over the house
For the past two or three days
As if looking for a pond
Or a friend
Or both.
If so, it is not likely
To find satisfaction hereabouts.
We are in the midst
Of the sere, parched
Desiccating days of August
And standing water is a mere figment
Of dusty-throated memory.
And as for an amigo
Well, the most we can offer
Are the two flamingos
Standing stolidly
Among the gnomes and toads
Beside the neighbor's emptied fountain
Erect and unmoving
And not even remotely convivial.

But perhaps the heron is not lost at all
Perhaps it is a greatly curious bird
Embarked upon an excursion
To explore the wide world
Beyond its marshland home
Of reeds and muck and mire.
Perhaps it is possessed
Of a restless spirit
Seeking new landscapes,
New vistas,
To nourish its imagination.

Whatever the reasons for its passing overhead
We are grateful for the flyby
And eager for frequent returns.
We live in an uncertaln world
And precarious times.
For example

Because of rainless weather
And increasingly extreme heat
Every day and night for the next few months
We will not stop worrying
About catastrophic conflagrations
Roaring hungrily down the forested mountain
To devour our homes.
So the wild and ancient grace
Of a heron in flight
Is a reminder
That even in perilous times
We must dare to take heart,
And an emblem
Of all that could be lost.

Yellow mushroom

A warm day in late January
No rain for two or three weeks
But the ground in the woods and hills
Is still satisfyingly muddy
And by a rotting log I find
A small yellow mushroom
Standing perfectly erect
Like a ballerina or a gymnast
Preparing to launch herself
Into the mild bright air.
But of course the lovely little fungus
Has no such idea
No plans to leap or twirl or dive,
For a mushroom understands
That one can also praise existence
By remaining perfectly quiet and still
With feet planted firmly
In moldering earth.

The wild beauty within

A small green heron is perched
On the power line
Above the neighbor's house
Looking as if it had placed itself there
To display for us
A moment of respite,
Of calm
In the midst of the storms
Assailing us right now—
COVID 19, punishing heat waves,
Rampant wildfires,
Political upheaval,
And our own fevered, baffled flailing
As we desperately seek to fathom and accomplish
The b est we can do in these times
For each other and ourselves.

The sky is an ominous smear of gray
Lightning flashes, thunder booms,
Brief showers come and go,
But not the steady downpour
That would make momentary optimists
Of us all.
No other birds are about
Just the little heron
Perfectly tranquil,
Poised within its own heron-ness
Unpestered by crows and jays,
But before we can fetch binoculars
For a closer look
It lifts itself up
Over houses and trees
Out of our story
And away.

We will try not to forget that heron-moment
Try to remember
The heron's exquisite pause
As a signifier
Of what we ourselves might do
To unite with the wild beauty within
As we prepare
For what storms may come.

Thank You

With overflowing love for the incandescent and unstoppable Cynthia.

With bottomless gratitude to the two dear friends willing to write kind words about these poems for the back cover:

Rod Anderson, a generous man of incomparable decency whose lively mind and wry humor always keep the conversation interesting;

Julie Searle, a woman with a capacious heart, a high-octane spirit, and a fierce respect for the dignity of children.

www.ingramcontent.com/pod-product-compliance
Lightning Source LLC
LaVergne TN
LVHW041558070426
835507LV00011B/1154